FREEWAY TO PERFECTION

A Collection of Mormon Cartoons by Calvin Grondahl

Published by The Sunstone Foundation, Salt Lake City, Utah

"YES SIR, I AM A MORMON. HOW COULD YOU TELL, SIR?"

"COME ON TONTO, GIVE THE INDIAN PLACEMENT PROGRAM A CHANCE."

"WE CAN COME BACK LATER IF THIS IS AN INCONVENIENT TIME."

"DID THE POOR ELDERS QUORUM PRESIDENT HAVE A BAD DAY?"

"THAT'S YOUR CONTINENT, KREBBS. WHAT HAPPENED?"

" ANYBODY FOR SECONDS ON FOOD STORAGE ? "

"AND YOU TOLD HIM WE'D PLACE THREE THOUSAND 'BOOKS OF MORMON' IN ONE DAY. ELDER, YOU'RE INSPIRING."

"AND WHEN YOUR RELIEF SOCIETY HEARD ABOUT YOUR OPERATION THEY RUSHED UP THREE DOZEN HOT ROLLS, THEY WERE DELICIOUS."

" WELL HARRY, I'LL GIVE YOU THIS MUCH — YOU ARE A SPIRITUAL GIANT. "

"IT'S A MIRACLE ELDER! YOUR PAMPHLETS AREN'T EVEN WET!"

"DEAR JOURNAL... MY FIRST DAY IN SCHOOL... MY ROOMMATE APPEARS TO BE A TRAVEL BROCHURE FOR SODOM & GOMORRAH.."

"DO IT RIGHT, YOU'RE MUCKING UP MY SPECIAL EFFECTS."

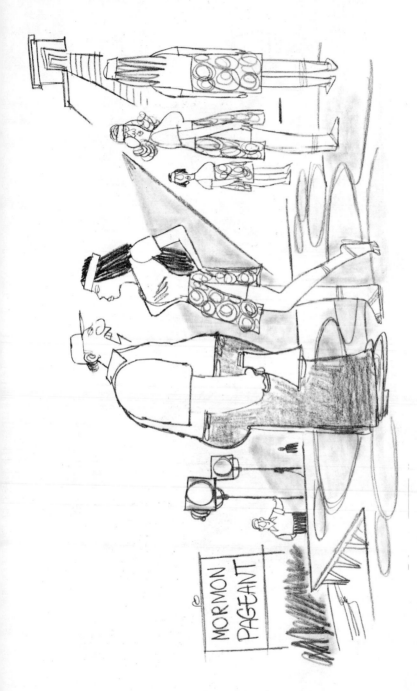

"YOU'RE SUPPOSED TO BE DANCING AT A LAMANITE BLOOD RITE, NOT AT A DISCO!"

"GENIUS HERE LOST THE MAP. NOW WE'RE NOT ONLY LOST, WE'RE REALLY LOST."

"NO, I DIDN'T READ IT. ALL YOUR PAMPHLETS LOOK ALIKE TO ME."

"THE SECRET OF A WARD LIBRARY IS ORGANIZATION, SISTER BENTROD."

"ALTHOUGH ONE IS NOT SUPPOSED TO KNOW THE EXACT DAY NOR HOUR OF THE SECOND COMING, I DID GIVE OUR NEW DATA STAR 2000 SERIES COMPUTER A CRACK AT IT."

"I GUESS THE 'BREASTPLATE OF RIGHTEOUSNESS' DOESN'T COVER THAT PART."

"TWO GENTLEMEN TO SEE YOU, SIR. IT'S THE DENOMINATION WITH THE FAMOUS GOLFERS."

"BRETHREN, IF YOU FEEL THAT YOU CAN'T ACHIEVE 100% HOME TEACHING, BROTHER CHANG—HERE HAS BEEN CALLED TO HELP YOU."

"AND AGAIN WE COUNSEL OUR MEMBERS TO STAY OUT OF DEBT."

"AND THEN HE SAID, 'SON, SEX IS NOT SECRET, IT'S SACRED AND TALKING ABOUT IT MAKES YOUR MOTHER FAINT.'"

"THEN I SAID TO MYSELF, WHAT WOULD THE SAVIOR DO?...
AND I FORGAVE HIM. THEN I ASKED MYSELF, WHAT WOULD
PORTER ROCKWELL DO? AND I SLUGGED HIM."

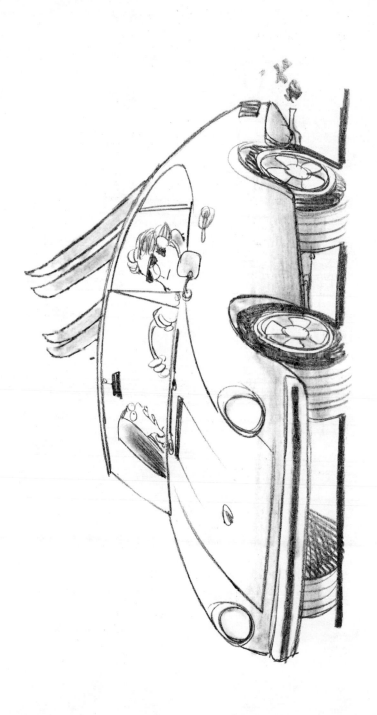

"I LOVE YOU CHUCK... BUT WILL YOUR PORSCHE 922 TAKE ME TO THE TEMPLE?"

"WE'RE STILL REHEARSING, SWEETHEART. YOUR SUPPER IS IN THE OVEN."

"I KNOW THAT I'M NOT SUPPOSED TO FISH ON SUNDAY, BUT I AM GIVING YOU TEN PERCENT."

" THEN AFTER HE SPENT TWO HOURS DISCUSSING HIS HIGH MORAL STANDARDS, HE WANTED TO SPEND TWO HOURS TESTING THEM. "

"OUR MISSIONARY SON WANTS US TO ADOPT A VILLAGE."

" HAROLD, I THINK YOU'VE DISCOVERED AN ANCIENT AMERICAN BAPTISMAL FONT ! "

"TODAY'S LESSON WILL BE ON REPENTANCE, WHICH WILL DETERIORATE INTO A DISCUSSION ON ANCIENT AMERICAN AIRFIELDS."

"YEAH, MY FOUR GENERATIONS CHART LOOKS JUST LIKE THAT ONE, BUT IT'S NOT CLUTTERED UP WITH ALL THOSE WORDS AND NUMBERS."

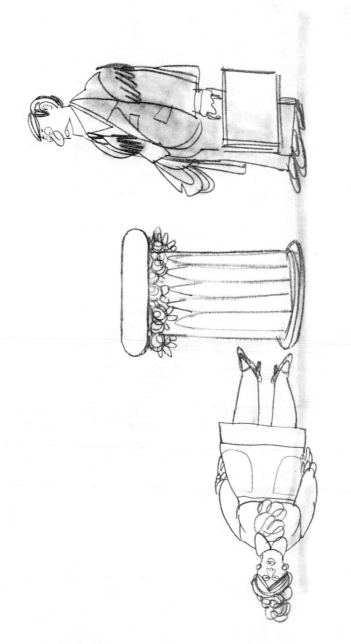

" SWEETHEART, 'YOU'VE FALLEN OFF YOUR PEDESTAL AGAIN!' "

" GOOD, THE KIDS HAVE T.R-ED THEIR SEMINARY TEACHER. THAT MEANS THEY ARE STARTING TO LIKE HIM. "

"AND YOU HAD TO PRAY FOR A _BIG_ FAMILY."

"IT WASN'T A 'SIGN OF THE TIMES' IT WAS JUST THE NEIGHBOR KIDS."

"IT COULD BE PART HUMAN, ELDER. WE'VE GOT TO TRACT IT OUT."

"DID ANYONE HERE REMEMBER TO BRING THE POISONED BIRDSEED?!"

"HE WAS 'DEAR JOHNED' THIS MORNING."

"I KNOW THE WORD OF WISDOM DOESN'T MENTION THE WORD 'FAT' SPECIFICALLY..."

"QUIT TORTURING YOURSELF ELDER. THERE'S NOT A McDONALDS WITHIN FIVE THOUSAND MILES OF THIS PLACE."

"I'D LIKE YOU TO MEET BROTHER ALEXANDER JONES — THE QUORUM'S TOKEN INTELLECTUAL."

"I'M SORRY DEAR... THE PRESSURES OF BEING PRESIDENT OF THE PRIMARY GOT TO ME."

"HOW CAN YOU SLEEP WITH SO MUCH SIN & PERVERSION IN THE WORLD ?"

"DON'T GIVE ME THAT. THE SACRED GROVE IS IN NEW YORK."

"SING A HYMN, ELDER... SING A HYMN."

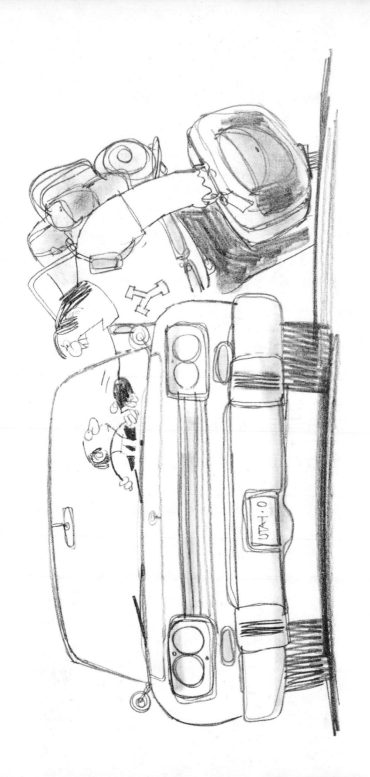

"I'M ONE OF THE THREE NEPHITES! AND I NEED YOUR CAR!"

"YOU MUST BE 1,5,7,2,3, DASH 22 DASH 42...WE RECEIVED YOUR RECORDS YESTERDAY. WELCOME TO THE WARD."

"... DEAR DIARY, TODAY THE SPIRIT GAVE ME THE 'GIFT OF TONGUES', AND
I INSULTED THREE FRENCH DOCKWORKERS. IT WAS THE WRONG SPIRIT."

"AND I THOUGHT MORONI WAS AN ITALIAN OPERA."

"DEAR, YOU'RE TALKING TO A MANNEQUIN WITH A PROJECTED SCREEN FACE."

"A CHOCOLATE BIRTHDAY BRICK, WHY ELDER, THIS IS JUST LIKE HOME."

"MISS TIPPETS WILL YOU STORE SIX HUNDRED POUNDS
OF WHEAT IN MY SWISS ACCOUNT."

" DOES YOUR PATRIARCHAL BLESSING REALLY SAY THAT YOU WILL MARRY A BEAUTIFUL AND SEXY WILDCAT? "

"NO, I DON'T HAVE MY TWO YEARS SUPPLY OF DRAMATIC READINGS."

"LET'S FACE IT YOU'VE DIRECTED TWENTY-SIX MORALLY CLEAN BOX OFFICE BOMBS."

ELDER, I'M GETTING SICK AND TIRED OF YOUR STUPID DOOR APPROACHES.

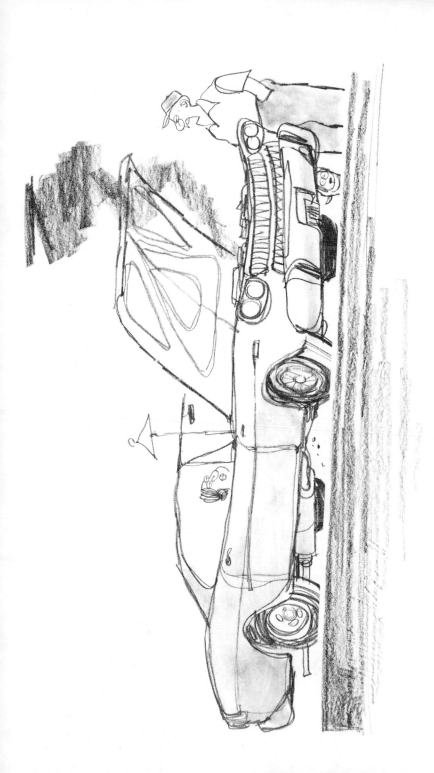

"I THINK IT JUST PASSED THROUGH THE VEIL AND WAS MET BY OUR OLD 51' CHEVY."

"WELL, I WAITED FOR YOUR SON FOR TWO YEARS, AND NOW HE TELLS ME HE'S CHANGED AND THAT CHANGES EVERYTHING. YOU'LL FIND HIM LOCKED IN YOUR TRUNK."

" NO, ELDER, REALLY...., I SAW AN EVIL SPIRIT."

"I'D LIKE TO PLAY SOMETHING WILDLY RADICAL IN THE SEVENTEENTH CENTURY WHICH IS NOW SPIRITUALLY ACCEPTABLE IN THE 20th."

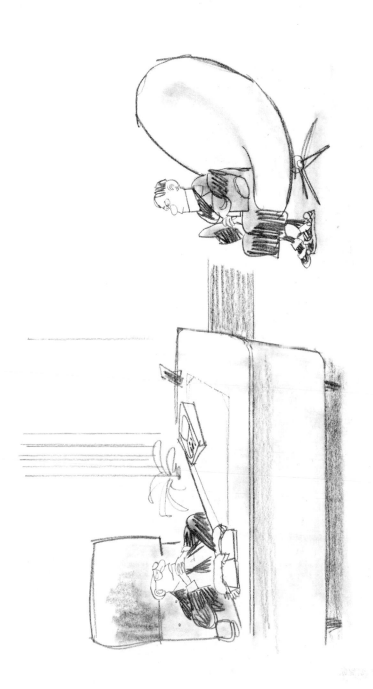

"ACTUALLY, WE HERE IN L.D.S. CHURCH FINANCE ARE NOT IN THE HABIT OF BUYING-OUT INSIGNIFICANT DENOMINATIONS."

" ELDER, PLEASE, SHE'S NOT INTERESTED. "

"AND I PAID YOU FIFTY BUCKS IN THE PRE-EXISTENCE NOT TO SHOW UP HERE."

"WE SORT OF MULTIPLIED AND REPLENISHED
THE EARTH, MARS AND HALF OF JUPITER."

WE NEED SOMETHING BEAUTIFUL AND INSPIRING, AND YET REFLECTS THE TASTE OF THE AMERICAN MIDDLE CLASS."

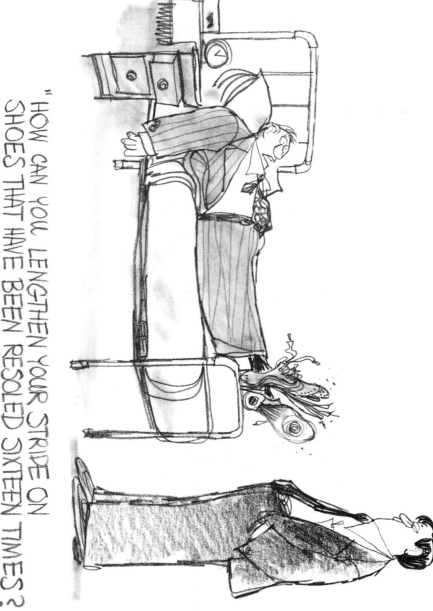

"HOW CAN YOU LENGTHEN YOUR STRIDE ON SHOES THAT HAVE BEEN RESOLED SIXTEEN TIMES?"

"THIS HIGH POINT IS WHEN WE SOLD THE DONNY OSMOND AUTOGRAPHS."

"FOR YEARS MARVIN AND I HAVE BEEN RATING THE TALKS FROM ONE TO TEN. WOULD YOU LIKE TO KNOW YOUR SCORE?"

"WE'RE ABOUT TO OPEN A NEW MISSION."

"COME ON, BROTHER YOUNG. WHERE'S YOUR STRONG PIONEER STOCK?"

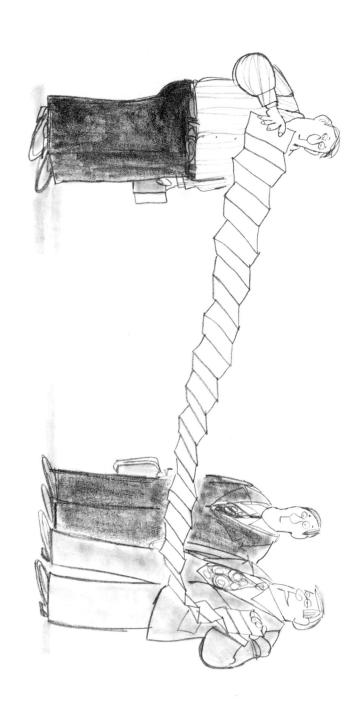

"AND WE'D LIKE TO LEAVE YOU THIS MAP ON 'WHERE DID I COME FROM?,, WHY AM I HERE?,, AND WHERE AM I GOING?'"

"YOU KNOW GETTING A TEMPLE RECOMMEND ISN'T LIKE GETTING A HUNTING LICENSE."

" ELDER, HOW MUCH DO YOU KNOW ABOUT OUTER SPACE?
...WOULD YOU LIKE TO KNOW MORE ? "

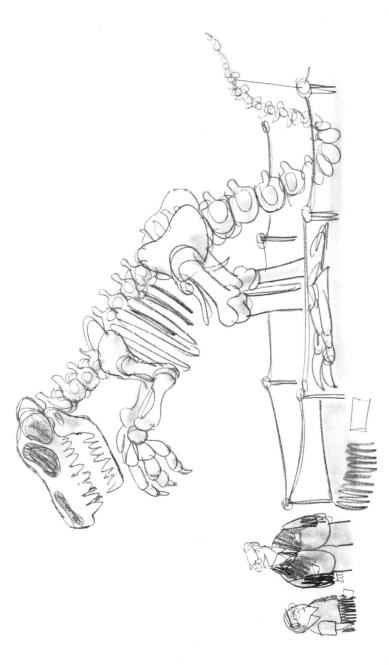

" HE SORT OF CREATED IT AND PLACED IT IN THE GARDEN SO ADAM WOULDN'T HAVE TO WORRY ABOUT BEING OVERRUN BY MICE."

"BUT ELDER, WE'VE JUST WON OUR OWN CHURCH!"

"THAT'S WILD WILLY; HE LIVES HERE IN THE UNDERGROUND VAULTS."

" MY ONLY HOPE IS THAT BRAZIL LEARNS ENGLISH WITHIN THE NEXT TWO MONTHS."

" YES, BUT I BELIEVE YOU TO BE THE PARENT AS FAR
AS YOU ARE TRANSLATED CORRECTLY. "

"WHY ANYONE WOULD WANT TO BE EQUAL TO YOU, I'LL NEVER KNOW."

" TONIGHT'S SPEAKER HAS SERVED IN THE CHURCH EDUCATION SYSTEM MOST OF HIS LIFE. HE HAS BEEN THE AUTHOR OF SUCH BOOKS AS, 'PROPHECY-KEY TO GOOD GARDENING.' "

"SOMEDAY MRS. SPACKLE, YOU'LL THANK US FOR TAKING YOUR CIGARETTES."

"WHENEVER YOU'RE DOWN THINK OF THE PROPHETS AND THEIR EXAMPLES OF COURAGE. THEN AGAIN NEAH NEVER FLUNKED OUT OF COLLEGE."

" WE'RE ONLY GOING TO CONVERT YOUR WHOLE COUNTRY, GENERAL. NOT CAUSE ANY TROUBLE."

SUNSTONE

Published six times yearly by the non-profit Sunstone Foundation, SUNSTONE seeks to examine the breadth of LDS experience and thought. Each issue includes a variety of personal essays, history, fiction, theology, social issues, humor, art, interviews, and more. In addition, SUNSTONE regularly publishes the best papers presented at the annual Sunstone Theological Symposium as well as the quarterly lectures of the B. H. Roberts Society.

SUNSTONE is a *must* for every thoughtful Mormon.

SPECIAL INTRODUCTORY OFFER

With every new subscription to SUNSTONE you can get an additional subscription to THE SUNSTONE REVIEW for only $4. THE SUNSTONE REVIEW readily puts the expanding Mormon community at your fingertips by collecting and condensing articles and features from hundreds of national and local publications and reviewing dozens of LDS-related books and cultural events.

1 YEAR OF SUNSTONE and THE SUNSTONE REVIEW

☐ $18 (a savings of $3.50)
☐ $14 for SUNSTONE magazine only
☐ $7.50 for THE SUNSTONE REVIEW only

☐ Enclosed $_____
☐ Bill me.

Name _____

Address _____

City/State/Zip _____

Offer applies to new subscriptions. Prices do not apply to foreign subscriptions.